A *LifeBuilder*

CW00919672

COLOSSIANS & PHILEMON

10 studies
for individuals or groups

Martha Reapsome

with notes for leaders

♨ Scripture Union is an international Christian charity working with churches in more than 130 countries providing resources to bring the good news about Jesus Christ to children, young people and families – and to encourage them to develop spiritually through the Bible and prayer. As well as coordinating a network of volunteers, staff and associates who run holidays, church-based events and school Christian groups, Scripture Union produces a wide range of publications and supports those who use their resources through training programmes.

Scripture Union, 207-209 Queensway, Bletchley, MK2 2EB, England.
e-mail: info@scriptureunion.org.uk
website: www.scriptureunion.org.uk

Scripture Union Australia: Locked Bag 2, Central Coast Business Centre, NSW 2252.
www.su.org.au

ISBN 978 1 85999 491 7

First published in the United States by InterVarsity Press 1989, revised in 2000.
First published in Great Britain by Scripture Union 2000, reprinted 2004, 2007, 2008.

British Library Cataloguing-in-Publication data: a catalogue record for this book is available from the British Library.

Printed in Singapore at Tien Wah Press.

Contents

Getting the Most Out of *Colossians & Philemon*

"More! More!" urged our son John when I laid down the spoon after feeding him.

"Again! Again!" pleaded our daughter Sara as I turned the last page in the book I was reading to her.

Their cries for more pudding or stories are echoed in our culture's search for more—more power, more money, more knowledge, more gadgets, more furniture, more clothes—more everything!

Books on self-improvement and success flood the market. Gurus gain eager followers by offering enlightenment, power and secret wisdom. Millions read horoscopes every day.

Not only in our society but also in the church, we cry for "more." If only we had more wisdom, more maturity, more power, more faith. To fill these needs we attend seminars, go to concerts, hear celebrity speakers and read their latest books.

Colossians was written to Christians with similar longings. They didn't know Who and what they already had. False teachers urged them to add rules, ascetic practices and new philosophies to their Christian faith. Then they would have fullness of life. Paul writes to satisfy their desire for more by showing that they already had fullness in Christ.

Paul never traveled to Colossae, a city in the Lycus River valley about a hundred miles east of Ephesus and twelve miles from Laodicea. But somehow he met Epaphras, the man who had taken the gospel to Colossae, and Philemon, the host for the local house church.

While in prison in Rome, Paul learned from Epaphras about the Colossian church and the pressures threatening their peace and stability. These "faithful brothers" had not turned away from faith in Christ. Paul's warm, friendly letter affirms their positive qualities and the changes in their lives. But he warns them against being deceived by "fine-sounding arguments" (2:4) or being captured by "hollow and deceptive philosophy, which depends on human tradition and on the basic principles of this world rather than on Christ" (2:8).

The temptation to add ascetic practices, regulations or "superior knowledge" threatened their dependence on Christ alone for the fullness of life they wanted. The early Gnostics boasted about a spiritual "fullness" not previously experienced. They promised to complete and perfect the simple and elementary faith introduced by Paul and Epaphras. They emphasized a deeper knowledge of God, reserved for a special few, and an experience of greater power.

Colossians is Paul's strongest declaration of the uniqueness and sufficiency of Christ, his full authority over all powers and the fullness of life he gives. Paul spells out the implications of this fullness of life again and again in the letter.

Like the Colossians, we are bombarded by longings for something more. But Paul thunders in Colossians, You already have fullness in Christ. Enjoy it! "For in Christ all the fullness of the Deity lives in bodily form, and you have been given fullness in Christ" (2:9-10).

The little book of Philemon is the only surviving letter of Paul to an individual friend and convert about a private matter. In it we learn that Onesimus, one of Philemon's slaves, had stolen from his master and run away to Rome. In that great city he met Paul and became a Christian. Under Roman law Philemon had the right to brand a returned slave and even kill him.

Paul applies what he wrote in Colossians: "Here there is no Greek or Jew. . . slave or free, but Christ is all, and is in all" (3:11). Philemon and Onesimus are given the chance to participate in a revolutionary new process for reconciliation.

The purpose of this guide is to help you discover the scope, reality and implications of the fullness of life you have in Christ. The first study gives you an overview of the tone and contents of the letter. The next eight studies help you explore and apply the main ideas of each section. Study ten examines Paul's letter to Philemon, which gives principles for mending broken relationships.

May Colossians and Philemon enlarge your appreciation of Jesus Christ and the fullness of life he has already given you. May you live out that fullness in joyful gratitude to him.

Suggestions for Individual Study

1. As you begin each study, pray that God will speak to you through his Word.

2. Read the introduction to the study and respond to the personal reflection question or exercise. This is designed to help you focus on God and on the theme of the study.

3. Each study deals with a particular passage—so that you can delve into the author's meaning in that context. Read and reread the passage to be studied. If you are studying a book, it will be helpful to read through the entire book prior to the first study. The questions are written using the language of the New International Version, so you may wish to use that version of the Bible. The New Revised Standard Version is also recommended.

4. This is an inductive Bible study, designed to help you discover for yourself what Scripture is saying. The study includes three types of questions. *Observation* questions ask about the basic facts: who, what, when, where and how. *Interpretation* questions delve into the meaning of the passage. *Application* questions help you discover the implications of the text for growing in Christ. These three keys unlock the treasures of Scripture.

Write your answers to the questions in the spaces provided or in a personal journal. Writing can bring clarity and deeper understanding of yourself and of God's Word.

5. It might be good to have a Bible dictionary handy. Use it to look up any unfamiliar words, names or places.

6. Use the prayer suggestion to guide you in thanking God for what you have learned and to pray about the applications that have come to mind.

7. You may want to go on to the suggestion under "Now or Later," or you may want to use that idea for your next study.

Suggestions for Members of a Group Study

1. Come to the study prepared. Follow the suggestions for individual study mentioned above. You will find that careful preparation will greatly enrich your time spent in group discussion.

2. Be willing to participate in the discussion. The leader of your group will not be lecturing. Instead, he or she will be encouraging the members of the group to discuss what they have learned. The leader will be asking the questions that are found in this guide.

3. Stick to the topic being discussed. Your answers should be based on the verses which are the focus of the discussion and not on outside authorities such as commentaries or speakers. These studies focus on a particular passage of Scripture. Only rarely should you refer to other portions of the Bible. This allows for everyone to participate in in-depth study on equal ground.

4. Be sensitive to the other members of the group. Listen attentively when they describe what they have learned. You may be surprised by their insights! Each question assumes a variety of answers. Many questions do not have "right" answers, particularly questions that aim at meaning or application. Instead the questions push us to explore the passage more thoroughly.

When possible, link what you say to the comments of others. Also, be affirming whenever you can. This will encourage some of the more hesitant members of the group to participate.

5. Be careful not to dominate the discussion. We are sometimes so eager to express our thoughts that we leave too little opportunity for others to respond. By all means participate! But allow others to also.

6. Expect God to teach you through the passage being discussed and through the other members of the group. Pray that you will have an enjoyable and profitable time together, but also that as a result of the study you will find ways that you can take action individually and/or as a group.

7. Remember that anything said in the group is considered confidential and should not be discussed outside the group unless specific permission is given to do so.

8. If you are the group leader, you will find additional suggestions at the back of the guide.

1

Letter from a Famous Stranger

Colossians 1—4

How exciting to get a celebrity's autograph! We love to retell the circumstances when we spotted him or her, how we approached him, what she said and how we felt as we floated away with the prize in hand.

GROUP DISCUSSION. Tell about a time you had an encounter with a famous person.

PERSONAL REFLECTION. Thank God for preserving this letter for your benefit. Ask him to increase your eagerness to know and apply the message of this letter to your life.

To the Colossians, Paul was somewhat of a celebrity. The Colossians had never met him. Yet instead of getting his autograph, they received an entire letter from him. In this study we'll read the letter they received. We'll get acquainted with these impressive Christians and the issues that prompted Paul's letter. We'll see those issues in the context of the whole letter. *Read Colossians 1—4.*

---

1. Imagine yourself as one of those new Christians crowded into a home to listen to this unexpected letter from Paul. What emotions would you feel while you're waiting for the others to arrive?

2. How would you describe the emotional tone of this letter?

3. How would you respond to a letter with the same tone?

4. What impresses you about these Colossian Christians?

5. What dangers does Paul warn against (2:8—3:11)?

If he were writing today, which dangers might he still include?

6. Into what main sections would you divide the letter?

What brief title would you give each section?

_____

7. Paul's theme statement is found in Colossians 2:9-10. What examples of this theme do you find in each section of the book?

_____

8. Which parts of the letter are the most encouraging to you, and why?

Which are the most confusing or troubling? Why?

_____

9. What characteristics of the Colossians do you want to see develop in your life or in your church?

Ask the Holy Spirit to help you discover and apply the truth of this letter.

Now or Later

To fully benefit from the central theme of Colossians, memorize 2:9-10. As you review the verses, ask God to help you see their implications in your life each day.

2

Thanks & Prayer

Colossians 1:1-14

"God bless Jennifer today" may be a typical prayer for a friend as she comes to mind. But what am I specifically asking for? How will I know if my prayer is answered? What difference would it make in Jennifer's life?

GROUP DISCUSSION. When you pray for another Christian, what do you usually say?

PERSONAL REFLECTION. How you feel when a friend tells you the specific things he or she notices and appreciates about you? Thank God for a friend who encourages you.

Paul begins his letter by telling the Colossians why he is thankful for them and what he asks God to do in them. Paul's example gives us a model for encouraging and praying for one another. *Read Colossians 1:1-14.*

1. What characteristics of the Colossians cause Paul to always be thankful for them (vv. 3-6)?

2. How are faith in Christ and love for other Christians related to the hope described in verse 5?

---

3. What examples of faith, love and hope have you seen in a group of Christians?

Who in your church or fellowship group could you affirm this week for demonstrating those qualities?

---

4. What impresses you about how the gospel was spreading (vv. 5-8)?

---

5. How have others helped you to hear and understand the truth about God's grace?

---

6. After affirming their strengths, in verses 9-14 Paul tells the Colossians what he prays for them. What are Paul's requests for how the Colossians would think and act?

---

7. Spiritual wisdom and understanding fill us with knowledge of God's will. From what less helpful sources do we try to find knowledge of God's will?

8. According to Paul, true knowledge leads to a "life worthy of the Lord" (v. 10). What qualities does such a life include (vv. 10-12)?

_____

9. In what specific ways do you see these qualities developing in your life?

_____

10. How does Paul graphically contrast our condition before and after we became Christians (vv. 12-14)?

_____

11. Reread verses 12-14 putting your name in each sentence. How would meditating on these verses help you to appreciate what God has done for you?

Pray for your church or fellowship group using Colossians 1:9-14 as your model.

Now or Later

Think of a friend, perhaps someone in your group, who demonstrates special qualities you appreciate. Following Paul's example, write a note or e-mail affirming him or her for those qualities. Or pray the prayer in Colossians 1:9-14 for a friend or for your group.

3

Jesus Is Supreme

Colossians 1:15-23

We frequently hear things like "All roads lead to God," "Everyone is trying to get to the same place," "Jesus is fine for you, but I don't buy it for myself," "Only bigots and fanatics label belief true or false."

GROUP DISCUSSION. How do you feel when you hear these popular points of view?

PERSONAL REFLECTION. Reflect on the problems you have encountered in helping someone understand why Jesus is the only way to God. Ask God to use this study to help you overcome these problems.

The Colossians heard "Worship Jesus—but not exclusively. Jesus is just one spirit among many to be worshiped." In this passage we'll study Paul's adamant declaration of Christ's supremacy over every being and idea that challenge his authority. *Read Colossians 1:15-23.*

1. Drawing from verses 15-18, make as many statements as you can about why Jesus is supreme. Begin each with "Christ is . . ."

2. What difficulties do you have in relating to an invisible God?

How has Jesus overcome those difficulties (v. 15)?

---

3. How do discoveries made through microscopes and telescopes add to your appreciation of Jesus' supremacy over nature (vv. 16-17)?

---

4. What does it mean that Christ is the "head of the body, the church" (v. 18)?

---

5. In what practical ways is Christ's headship evident in your church?

---

6. How did some recent choice you made about your time or money reflect Christ's place in your life?

---

7. Bad news: Our sin makes us enemies of God, alienating us from him. Good news: God chose to take the initiative to reconcile us to himself or to make peace with us. How do you respond to knowing what it cost God to reconcile us sinners to himself (vv. 19-22)?

8. How can these verses help you explain why Jesus is the only way to God?

---

9. What emotions do the words *reconciled, holy in his sight, without blemish* and *free from accusation* (vv. 22-23) evoke in you?

---

10. How might those words appeal to some unspoken needs of friends you want to introduce to Jesus?

How do they affect your determination to continue firm in your faith in Christ?

Thank and worship Jesus Christ for who he is and what he has done for you and your friends who don't yet know him.

Now or Later

For more help in discussing Jesus with your friends, read the booklet *Absolute Truth?* by Mark Ashton (InterVarsity Press).

4

Growing Pains

Colossians 1:24—2:5

For a whole year a young man lived in isolation on a remote Arctic mountain. He risked his life on the flight in. And he risked his life daily as he walked over trails of thin ice (which gave way when he struggled under a heavy backpack). He shared his cold tent with mice and mosquitoes. He experimented with a diet of boiled, fried or charred mice. Why would anyone willingly subject himself to such hardships? Farley Mowat had a goal. He wanted to learn the relationship between the wolves and the diminishing caribou herds.

GROUP DISCUSSION. What goal has been compelling enough to make you willing to suffer to reach it?

PERSONAL REFLECTION. Consider where you have invested time, energy and money in the last two years. What do those investments reveal about your goals? What changes would you like to make?

In this study Paul describes his compelling goal, his struggles and his resources to reach it. *Read Colossians 1:24—2:5.*

1. How does Paul define God's commission to him (1:24-29)?

2. In the New Testament the term *mystery* refers not to something mysterious but to something previously hidden that God now wishes to make clear. What is the mystery that represents the "word of God in its fullness" (1:26-27; 2:2-3)?

---

3. Why would this mystery be startling to both Jews and Gentiles in the Colossian church?

---

4. What feelings does this idea of "Christ in you" arouse? (Consider the description of Christ you studied in Colossians 1:15-20.)

---

5. Paul's ultimate goal includes more than just disclosing a mystery. He struggles to present everyone perfect or mature in Christ (1:28). In addition to prayer (1:9), what does Paul do to achieve that goal (1:28-29)?

---

6. Which of these means has God used to help you toward maturity in Christ?

7. Paul describes specific marks of Christian maturity. Which of these marks in 2:2-5 do you see developing in yourself?

Which would you like to develop?

---

8. The Gnostics taught that secret knowledge was the key to salvation and spiritual maturity. Paul's description of Christ (2:3-4) could protect the Colossians from the "fine-sounding arguments." What "fine-sounding arguments" today lure us away from Christ and hinder our spiritual maturity?

---

9. How can we keep our Christian commitment as focused as Farley Mowat's commitment to the wolves?

Ask God to help you refocus your attention on Christ and on his goals for you.

Now or Later

Review the marks of Christian maturity you identified in question 7. Thank God for the marks you see now in your life. Ask for grace in your struggle to continue to grow.

5

No Additions
Needed

Colossians 2:6-23

Kim Yeng and his family celebrated the day they became American citizens. Now they were no longer refugees but free citizens with full privileges and endless opportunities. Kim wanted to be sure they were unmistakable Americans. So he erected a flag pole in the front yard and flew the flag every day. The children wore red, white and blue outfits to school. Hamburgers and potatoes replaced egg rolls and rice for dinner. Though they were already citizens, Kim kept adding ways to make them look and feel more like citizens.

GROUP DISCUSSION. How have you heard this sentence completed: To be spiritually mature, a Christian must . . . ?

PERSONAL REFLECTION. Thank God for all you have because you have received Christ. Recall what that includes from Colossians 1:15-22 and 2:2-3.

In this passage Paul questions the Colossians about the foolish human additions they are making to what they already have in Christ. *Read Colossians 2:6-15.*

---

1. How do each of the images in verse 7—*rooted, built up, strengthened* and *overflowing*—help you picture true spiritual growth?

Which of these connects your experience? How?

___

2. Verse 8 gives the first real glimpse of the heresy being taught to the Colossians. What was wrong with this false teaching?

___

3. According to the false teachers, believing in Christ was a good beginning, but you must do more: honor other spiritual beings, observe special days and deny yourself certain foods. To protect Christians from such heresies, Paul declares in verse 10, "You have been given fullness in Christ." The New Living Translation says, "You are complete through your union with Christ." How do you respond to the idea of being *complete* or having *fullness* in Christ?

___

4. In verses 11-15 Paul describes some of what "fullness in Christ" means. Think about your most basic needs—acceptance, belonging, significance, forgiveness, purpose, love. Which of these needs has Jesus' death, burial and resurrection fulfilled for you?

___

5. Why is it important for Jesus to take care of our sinful nature (v. 11) as well as our sins (v. 13)?

6. Silently read verses 9-15 inserting your name every time Paul says "you" or "us." How do these facts affect your view of yourself?

7. *Read Colossians 2:16-23.* What "shadows" were the Colossians adding to the "reality" they had found in Christ (vv. 16-17, 20-23)?

What "shadows" are we tempted to add today?

8. Why do such humanly conceived additions appeal to us (vv. 18-19, 22-23)?

9. Why are legalism and asceticism useless in making us spiritually mature or more complete in Christ (vv. 22-23)?

10. What does it mean to "receive Christ Jesus as Lord" (v. 6)?

What has this passage revealed to you about Christ's place in your life?

Use the following hymn as a prayer of thanks for your fullness and completeness in Christ.

> Complete in Thee! no work of mine
> May take, dear Lord, the place of Thine;
> Thy blood hath pardon bought for me,
> And I am now complete in Thee.
>
> Complete in Thee! no more shall sin,
> Thy grace hath conquered, reign within;
> Thy voice shall bid the tempter flee,
> And I shall stand complete in Thee.
>
> Complete in Thee! each want supplied,
> And no good thing to me denied;
> Since Thou my portion, Lord, wilt be,
> I ask no more, complete in Thee.
>
> Dear Saviour! when before thy bar
> All tribes and tongues assembled are,
> Among Thy chosen will I be,
> At Thy right hand complete in Thee.
>
> Aaron R. Wolfe (1821-1902)

Now or Later

Read the hymn each day, allowing the wonder of being complete in Jesus to saturate your heart and mind. Review Colossians 2:9-10 from memory.

6

New Life

Have you seen pictures of marathon runners? Concentration and determination seem to ooze from every pore. These people set their hearts and minds on one thing—finishing the race. They focus on the next step, the next checkpoint, until the race is complete. They shed pounds, unnecessary clothing or anything else that might slow them down. Attach their official number and they are ready to run.

GROUP DISCUSSION. As a child, how did setting your heart on a certain toy or gift affect how you acted and what you thought about?

PERSONAL REFLECTION. When you are alone and don't have to focus on anything in particular, what do you think about? What are your most frequent emotions? Talk to God about what you recognize about where your mind and heart are set.

As Christians we are to live like marathon runners. We are to take off anything that slows us down and set our hearts and minds on the finish line. *Read Colossians 3:1-11.*

---

1. What reasons and benefits does Paul give for setting our hearts and minds on Christ (vv. 1, 3-4)?

2. What do you think Paul means by "things above" and "earthly things" (vv. 1-2)?

3. In what kinds of situations are you tempted to set your heart and mind on earthy things?

4. How can we set our *hearts* and *minds* on things above rather than on earthly things?

5. Just as runners strip themselves of all unnecessary weight, Christians must shed whatever weights them down. What do the things we are to "put to death" have in common (v. 5)?

6. In what sense does greed equal idolatry (vv. 5-7)?

7. How can we keep God's perspective on immorality and greed when our culture accepts them as normal?

---

8. Our old ways of reacting are compared to a garment we took off when we received Christ (vv. 8-10). Why is each type of behavior inconsistent with our new life in Christ?

---

9. How does falling back into these old motives or actions in verses 5 and 8-9 affect you and your relationships to others?

---

10. We may still struggle with these sins, but what resources can help us to change (vv. 9-11)?

How are these resources better than "grit your teeth" determination and "trying harder"?

_____

11. In verse 11 Paul lists the distressing divisions between people in the Colossian culture. If he were writing today, what division do you think he would name?

_____

12. How has becoming aware of Christ in other Christians (perhaps where you didn't expect it) encouraged you in your faith?

Pray for help in the area where you feel weak—setting your heart and mind on Christ, shedding specific attitudes and actions. Spend time thanking God for the changes he has already made in you.

Now or Later

Thank God that you are continually being renewed as you learn more and more about Christ (3:10 NLT). What are the things God is doing in you? Keep a list as an ongoing source of encouragement.

7

New Lifestyle

Colossians 3:12-17

Marathon runners not only shed anything that might slow them down, they also dress carefully. They choose the best running shoes and the most comfortable shorts and shirt. Golfers wear visors to protect their eyes from the sun and spiked shoes to keep them from slipping while hitting the ball. Taking part in different hobbies and social groups requires specific dress and behavior.

GROUP DISCUSSION. When you were a child, what was one behavior your parents insisted on just because you were a member of their family?

PERSONAL REFLECTION. Think of a Christian whose life you admire. What character qualities attract you? What role does thankfulness have in their lives?

After telling us what to get rid of, Paul now speaks about the new clothes we are to wear because of our new life in Christ. *Read Colossians 3:12-17.*

---

1. What clues do you get regarding Paul's feelings about the Colossians from these verses?

2. Why does Paul begin by reminding us of who we are in God's sight (v. 12)?

3. How does the description "God's chosen people, holy and dearly loved" (3:12) compare to your view of yourself?

4. Review 1:12-14 and 2:9-10. What do these verses contribute to your identity?

5. If you and your Christian friends put on the "new clothes" of *compassion, kindness, humility, gentleness* and *patience*, what effect do you think it would have on your family, neighbors and coworkers?

6. Paul recognizes that grievances occur even in the church. How do his instructions for handling grievances differ from the way our culture handles them (vv. 13-14)?

———————————————————————————————

7. How could conflicts be better managed if peace ruled (literally, "functioning like an umpire") in our hearts (v. 15)?

———————————————————————————————

8. How can we let the word of Christ *dwell* in us richly (v.16; see also Ephesians 5:18-20)?

———————————————————————————————

9. What opportunities exist in your church or group to teach, admonish and sing as described in verse 16?

What opportunities would you like to create?

10. What is the significance of thankfulness that Paul would command it three different ways (vv. 15, 16, 17)?

---

11. How would doing everything "in the name of the Lord Jesus" transform what you have to say and do this week (v. 17)?

---

12. In contrast to the rules mentioned in 2:16-23, how are these "new clothes" appropriate expressions of the fullness we have in Christ?

Thank God that you are his chosen people, holy and dearly loved. Ask for grace and power to "dress" appropriately. Confess your disobedience as God convicts you.

Now or Later

Memorize 3:17. Reflect each evening on the difference it makes to speak and act in the name of the Lord Jesus.

8

At Home &
on the Job

Colossians 3:18—4:1

Factory workers in the Philippines had been meeting for months for a lunch-hour Bible study. One day the supervisor came to the leader and asked, "Could you start some more Bible studies in the factory? The men in the study have become the best workers on my shift." The change in the factory workers wouldn't have surprised the apostle Paul.

GROUP DISCUSSION. What attitudes have you seen in a family or on the job that you would label as "Christian"?

PERSONAL REFLECTION. Reflect on God's goodness in creating families for our good. Thank him for your parents and extended family, though no one has perfect parents. Ask the Holy Spirit to teach you what you need to learn from this study.

In this section of Colossians, Paul instructs us about the distinctive attitudes and behavior that should mark Christians at home and on the job. *Read Colossians 3:18—4:1.*

---

1. How do Paul's commands to wives-husbands, children-fathers and slaves-masters sound like the opposites of our tendencies?

2. The wife is to submit to the husband "as is fitting in the Lord" (v.18). From what you learned in Colossians 3:5-17, what would that kind of submission include?

What would it not include?

3. The husband is to love his wife and not be harsh with her (v. 19). How would Colossians 3:12-17 help him understand what that love looks like in actions and attitudes?

4. These commands to submit and love are unconditional, that is, not dependent on the behavior of the spouse. What objections might a person raise to these instructions?

5. Why do you think the basic command to children is "Obey your parents" (v. 20)?

6. Fathers are told what *not* to do: embitter or discourage their children (v. 21). How can parents teach obedience without embittering or discouraging their children?

---

7. What difference would it make in family relationships if the members wanted to please the Lord (v. 20) and encourage each other (v. 21)?

---

8. Paul turns from relationships in the family to relationships with slaves in the home and workplace. His instructions to both slaves and masters must have sounded totally countercultural. When and how are slaves to obey their masters (vv. 22-25)?

With what motives?

---

9. What would it demand of a master to "provide your slaves with what is right and fair" (4:1)?

---

10. How should knowing that he has "a Master in heaven" affect a master's attitude toward himself and his slaves (3:25—4:1)?

---

11. If Paul wrote these instructions today, he would address employees and employers. What specific applications to motives and actions could you make in your workplace or vocation (3:22—4:1)?

Pray that your life will demonstrate your desire to please and honor the Lord Jesus at home and on the job.

Now or Later

Select one of the instructions addressed to you in this passage. Ask for wisdom and grace in applying that principle in your home or on the job this week. If you are studying in a group, report back on your efforts, your feelings and any reactions you encounter to your behavior.

9

Making the Most of Opportunities

Colossians 4:2-18

No one ever becomes a Christian by just watching how a Christian lives. An observer might think the Christian is earning his way to heaven by trying to be good. How could anyone ever guess how to become a Christian? Debating whether what we say or how we live is more important in witnessing is like asking which leg is more important for walking.

GROUP DISCUSSION. What emotions or associations does the word *witnessing* evoke in you?

PERSONAL REFLECTION. Reflect on one piece of advice about witnessing that someone has given to you. If you used it, what were the results? If you haven't used it, why not?

In this study Paul shows that witnessing is an interplay between prayer, living and speaking. His closing greetings illustrate many ways Christians help and encourage each other. *Read Colossians 4:2-6.*

---

1. Based on what you have read in Colossians, what are we to be watchful and thankful for (v. 2)?

2. In this section Paul teaches us how to speak to God about people and how to speak to people about God. Why would he tell us to *devote* ourselves to prayer (v. 2)?

3. Paul might have asked the church to pray for his release from prison. What requests does he make instead (vv. 3-4)? Why?

4. Since God is the one who opens doors for the gospel, take time now to pray these requests for your pastor, a missionary you know and yourself (vv. 3-4).

5. In verses 5-6 Paul gives us advice about the way we live and converse with non-Christians (vv. 5-6). In what ways might you "be wise in the way you act toward outsiders" and "make the most of every opportunity" (v. 5)?

6. How would conversation "always full of grace, seasoned with salt"

(v. 6) prompt questions from non-Christians?

7. How would it change your attitude toward witnessing if each day you expected questions about your wise actions and gracious, salty speech?

8. *Read Colossians 4:7-18.* Paul concludes this letter with numerous personal messages and greetings. What qualities in people does Paul affirm?

Which of these qualities do you wish were said of you?

9. You'll meet Onesimus, who was Philemon's runaway slave (v. 9), and Archippus, Philemon's son (v. 17), again in the next study. How might Paul's words make each one feel about himself and the other?

---

10. Epaphras, who had taken the gospel to the Colossians (1:7-8), is commended for his continuing concern for them. What impresses you about his prayer (v. 12)?

---

11. From what you've learned about the problems at Colossae, why are his requests particularly appropriate?

---

12. How would you like to see your prayer life changed by the themes in this study—or in the whole book of Colossians?

Ask for open doors to witness for Jesus and wisdom to live and speak the message clearly.

Now or Later

Following the example of Paul's friends, look for specific opportunities this week to encourage or comfort a fellow Christian.

10

Mending Fractured Relationships

Philemon 1-25

Dave and Andy enjoyed a prosperous business partnership for several years. Their families became close friends, sharing vacations made possible by their growing computer business. Then one day Andy disappeared—along with the company bank account. Dave lost his friend, his business and his home. Three years later Andy returned, having squandered the money but having found Christ. Could Dave forgive him? Could they ever be friends again?

GROUP DISCUSSION. Recall a time when you wanted to restore a broken relationship. What were some of your fears in approaching the situation?

PERSONAL REFLECTION. Thank the Lord Jesus for being your mediator to restore your relationship to God. Ask for honesty and humility in recognizing your part in any broken relationship.

In Paul's letter to Philemon you'll find principles for bringing reconciliation between two Christians who know the pain of wronging another and being wronged. *Read Philemon 1-25.*

1. Based on what you have read, how would you reconstruct the events that led up to this letter?

2. What impresses you about Philemon's character from verses 4-7?

What aspect of Philemon's character would you most like to grow in yourself?

3. Having described Philemon's loving character, Paul appeals to him on the basis of love (v. 9). Paul reminds Philemon that he could *order* him to do what he ought to do (v. 8). If we lack love for a person, why must we still be willing to forgive and accept him or her?

4. In what ways has Onesimus changed since running away from Philemon (vv. 10-16)? How might this help in the reconciliation process?

5. What will it require of Onesimus to return to Philemon?

6. What will it require of Philemon to do what Paul asks?

---

7. In what ways does Paul function as a mediator between these two men?

---

8. That this letter was kept and included in the Bible indicates that Philemon did welcome Onesimus as a brother. How would their slave-master relationship be changed? (Remember Colossians 3:11 and 3:22—4:1.)

How would it be the same?

---

9. What principles in this letter could you use for mending a fractured relationship?

Pray for God's grace to follow these principles in a situation where you may be an "Onesimus" or "Philemon" or "Paul."

Now or Later

Paul intervened to restore these two brothers in Christ. If you are aware of a Christian friend who needs to restore a relationship, consider how you could offer help.

Leader's Notes

MY GRACE IS SUFFICIENT FOR YOU. (2 COR 12:9)

Leading a Bible discussion can be an enjoyable and rewarding experience. But it can also be *scary*—especially if you've never done it before. If this is your feeling, you're in good company. When God asked Moses to lead the Israelites out of Egypt, he replied, "O Lord, please send someone else to do it"! (Ex 4:13). It was the same with Solomon, Jeremiah and Timothy, but God helped these people in spite of their weaknesses, and he will help you as well.

You don't need to be an expert on the Bible or a trained teacher to lead a Bible discussion. The idea behind these inductive studies is that the leader guides group members to discover for themselves what the Bible has to say. This method of learning will allow group members to remember much more of what is said than a lecture would.

These studies are designed to be led easily. As a matter of fact, the flow of questions through the passage from observation to interpretation to application is so natural that you may feel that the studies lead themselves. This study guide is also flexible. You can use it with a variety of groups—student, professional, neighborhood or church groups. Each study takes forty-five to sixty minutes in a group setting.

There are some important facts to know about group dynamics and encouraging discussion. The suggestions listed below should enable you to effectively and enjoyably fulfill your role as leader.

Preparing for the Study

1. Ask God to help you understand and apply the passage in your own life. Unless this happens, you will not be prepared to lead others. Pray too for the various members of the group. Ask God to open your hearts to the message of his Word and motivate you to action.

2. Read the introduction to the entire guide to get an overview of the entire book and the issues which will be explored.

3. As you begin each study, read and reread the assigned Bible passage to familiarize yourself with it.

4. This study guide is based on the New International Version of the Bible. It will help you and the group if you use this translation as the basis for your study and discussion.

5. Carefully work through each question in the study. Spend time in meditation and reflection as you consider how to respond.

6. Write your thoughts and responses in the space provided in the study guide. This will help you to express your understanding of the passage clearly.

7. It might help to have a Bible dictionary handy. Use it to look up any unfamiliar words, names or places. (For additional help on how to study a passage, see chapter five of *How to Lead a LifeGuide Bible Study*, InterVarsity Press.)

8. Consider how you can apply the Scripture to your life. Remember that the group will follow your lead in responding to the studies. They will not go any deeper than you do.

9. Once you have finished your own study of the passage, familiarize yourself with the leader's notes for the study you are leading. These are designed to help you in several ways. First, they tell you the purpose the study guide author had in mind when writing the study. Take time to think through how the study questions work together to accomplish that purpose. Second, the notes provide you with additional background information or suggestions on group dynamics for various questions. This information can be useful when people have difficulty understanding or answering a question. Third, the leader's notes can alert you to potential problems you may encounter during the study.

10. If you wish to remind yourself of anything mentioned in the leader's notes, make a note to yourself below that question in the study.

Leading the Study

1. Begin the study on time. Open with prayer, asking God to help the group to understand and apply the passage.

2. Be sure that everyone in your group has a study guide. Encourage the group to prepare beforehand for each discussion by reading the introduction to the guide and by working through the questions in the study.

3. At the beginning of your first time together, explain that these studies are meant to be discussions, not lectures. Encourage the members of the group to participate. However, do not put pressure on those who may be hesitant to speak during the first few sessions. You may want to suggest the fol-

lowing guidelines to your group.

☐ Stick to the topic being discussed.

☐ Your responses should be based on the verses which are the focus of the discussion and not on outside authorities such as commentaries or speakers.

☐ These studies focus on a particular passage of Scripture. Only rarely should you refer to other portions of the Bible. This allows for everyone to participate in in-depth study on equal ground.

☐ Anything said in the group is considered confidential and will not be discussed outside the group unless specific permission is given to do so.

☐ We will listen attentively to each other and provide time for each person present to talk.

☐ We will pray for each other.

4. Have a group member read the introduction at the beginning of the discussion.

5. Every session begins with a group discussion question. The question or activity is meant to be used before the passage is read. The question introduces the theme of the study and encourages group members to begin to open up. Encourage as many members as possible to participate, and be ready to get the discussion going with your own response.

This section is designed to reveal where our thoughts or feelings need to be transformed by Scripture. That is why it is especially important not to read the passage before the discussion question is asked. The passage will tend to color the honest reactions people would otherwise give because they are, of course, supposed to think the way the Bible does.

You may want to supplement the group discussion question with an icebreaker to help people to get comfortable. See the community section of *Small Group Idea Book* for more ideas.

You also might want to use the personal reflection question with your group. Either allow a time of silence for people to respond individually or discuss it together.

6. Have a group member (or members if the passage is long) read aloud the passage to be studied. Then give people several minutes to read the passage again silently so that they can take it all in.

7. Question 1 will generally be an overview question designed to briefly survey the passage. Encourage the group to look at the whole passage, but try to avoid getting sidetracked by questions or issues that will be addressed later in the study.

8. As you ask the questions, keep in mind that they are designed to be used just as they are written. You may simply read them aloud. Or you may prefer to express them in your own words.

There may be times when it is appropriate to deviate from the study guide. For example, a question may have already been answered. If so, move on to the next question. Or someone may raise an important question not covered in the guide. Take time to discuss it, but try to keep the group from going off on tangents.

9. Avoid answering your own questions. If necessary, repeat or rephrase them until they are clearly understood. Or point out something you read in the leader's notes to clarify the context or meaning. An eager group quickly becomes passive and silent if they think the leader will do most of the talking.

10. Don't be afraid of silence. People may need time to think about the question before formulating their answers.

11. Don't be content with just one answer. Ask, "What do the rest of you think?" or "Anything else?" until several people have given answers to the question.

12. Acknowledge all contributions. Try to be affirming whenever possible. Never reject an answer. If it is clearly off-base, ask, "Which verse led you to that conclusion?" or again, "What do the rest of you think?"

13. Don't expect every answer to be addressed to you, even though this will probably happen at first. As group members become more at ease, they will begin to truly interact with each other. This is one sign of healthy discussion.

14. Don't be afraid of controversy. It can be very stimulating. If you don't resolve an issue completely, don't be frustrated. Move on and keep it in mind for later. A subsequent study may solve the problem.

15. Periodically summarize what the group has said about the passage. This helps to draw together the various ideas mentioned and gives continuity to the study. But don't preach.

16. At the end of the Bible discussion you may want to allow group members a time of quiet to work on an idea under "Now or Later." Then discuss what you experienced. Or you may want to encourage group members to work on these ideas between meetings. Give an opportunity during the session for people to talk about what they are learning.

17. Conclude your time together with conversational prayer, adapting the prayer suggestion at the end of the study to your group. Ask for God's help in following through on the commitments you've made.

18. End on time.

Many more suggestions and helps are found in *How to Lead a LifeGuide Bible Study*.

Components of Small Groups
A healthy small group should do more than study the Bible. There are four
components to consider as you structure your time together.
   Nurture. Small groups help us to grow in our knowledge and love of God.
Bible study is the key to making this happen and is the foundation of your
small group.
   Community. Small groups are a great place to develop deep friendships
with other Christians. Allow time for informal interaction before and after
each study. Plan activities and games that will help you get to know each
other. Spend time having fun together—going on a picnic or cooking dinner
together.
   Worship and prayer. Your study will be enhanced by spending time praising
God together in prayer or song. Pray for each other's needs—and keep track
of how God is answering prayer in your group. Ask God to help you to apply
what you are learning in your study.
   Outreach. Reaching out to others can be a practical way of applying what
you are learning, and it will keep your group from becoming self-focused.
Host a series of evangelistic discussions for your friends or neighbors. Clean
up the yard of an elderly friend. Serve at a soup kitchen together, or spend a
day working on a Habitat house.
   Many more suggestions and helps in each of these areas are found in *Small
Group Idea Book.* Information on building a small group can be found in
Small Group Leaders' Handbook and *The Big Book on Small Groups* (both from
InterVarsity Press). Reading through one of these books would be worth your
time.

Study 1. Colossians 1—4. A Letter from a Famous Stranger.
Purpose: To get an overview of Paul's letter to this church he has never visited.
Introduction. Encourage the group to listen to the letter as though they were
members of the church in Colossae. One person might read the whole letter
aloud, or four people might read one chapter each. Hearing different voices
avoids monotony and involves more people.
Question 3. If the group needs help, you might suggest that letters can be
friendly, accusing, emotional, harsh, patronizing and so on.
Question 4. Encourage several brief answers, but don't try to be exhaustive.
The ideas will be dealt with in detail in later studies.
Question 6. The purpose of this question is to stimulate thinking and discussion about the main ideas in Colossians. The group may express them in different terms.

Question 7. Encourage the group to identify the implications of the theme of fullness and completeness in the sections they titled.

Question 8. Looking at the letter for its benefits to you will increase anticipation of future studies. You might want to list the confusing and troubling ideas to be sure the group examines them carefully when you come to them.

Question 9. Help the group to be honest and specific. They may find it harder to see their strengths than their problems.

Study 2. Colossians 1:1-14. Thanks & Prayer.

Purpose: To develop patterns for praying and for affirming other Christians.

Question 1. Encourage the group to state the characteristics in their own words. This will help draw out their significance.

Question 2. Paul affirms their faith, love and hope, but in contrast to the false teachers he does not mention knowledge. Their hope is in what God has done and prepared for them, not their superior knowledge.

Question 3. Ask for specific examples. Don't accept vague generalities or clichés.

Question 4. In your preparation observe carefully all the facts you can about how the gospel was spread. If the group misses some, you might ask, "What does verse____add to what we've already discussed?" Don't answer the question yourself but help the group to dig for answers. Paul's statement "all over the world" (v. 6) is an example of hyperbole, a deliberate exaggeration for dramatic effect. In the three decades since Pentecost the gospel had spread to every part of the Roman Empire.

Question 6. People may divide the requests differently, seeing various connections. But keep refining until you have a list of at least six or seven specific requests you could pray for a friend.

Question 7. Using the very terminology of those who are trying to lead the Colossians astray, Paul prays for their full knowledge of the will of God. F. F. Bruce writes: "This epistle (like that to the Ephesians) has much to say about 'knowledge' as a means of promoting Christian life. But the 'knowledge' of which the apostle speaks is no merely intellectual exercise, no theosophical gnosis such as was affected by the teachers who were leading the Colossians astray. He wishes to impress his readers with the character and importance of true knowledge before drawing their attention to the dangers of that 'knowledge falsely so called' which was being pressed on them. . . . Right knowledge, according to Paul, leads to right behaviour" (*The Epistles of Paul to the Ephesians and to the Colossians*, The New International Commentary on the New Testament [Grand Rapids, Mich.: Eerdmans, 1957], pp. 185-86).

In the second part of this question, avoid a long description of all the excesses people have heard. The point is to think of ways we substitute human and cultural wisdom for spiritual wisdom.

Question 8. A life worthy of the Lord includes fruitful activity in all kinds of good works. Note the progressive thought here: knowledge of God promotes service (vv. 9-10), service is repaid by strength (v. 11), and all is crowned by thanksgiving (v. 12). (See F. F. Bruce, *The International Bible Commentary* [Grand Rapids, Mich.: Zondervan, 1986], p. 1454).

Question 10. Redemption (v. 14), "a term that speaks of a release brought about by the payment of a price, was used of the deliverance of slaves from bondage or of prisoners of war from captivity" (Curtis Vaughan, *Colossians*, The Expositor's Bible Commentary [Grand Rapids, Mich.: Zondervan, 1978], p. 180).

Question 11. The group might read verses 12-14 aloud together, each member substituting his or her own name. Allow time for the group to draw the connections between what God has already done and what we need him to do for us today.

Prayer. You might ask each member of the group to select one item from verses 9-14 and use it to pray for the person on their right. Give the group time to choose a request before you pray. You can model by praying for the person on your right.

Study 3. Colossians 1:15-23. Jesus Is Supreme.

Purpose: To understand that Jesus Christ is supreme because of who he is and what he did. To encourage worship of Jesus and sharing of the good news.

Question 1. Notice that Paul uses the words *all* or *everything* eight times in six verses (vv. 15-20) in order to stress Christ's supremacy over all.

The phrase "firstborn over all creation" (v. 15) might be a problem to some in the group. Some cults use it to say Jesus was created and therefore is not God. However, "the term *first-born* is commonly used to mean 'supreme' or 'sovereign,' that is, 'having the rights of the first-born.' The best illustration of this usage is Psalm 89:27, where God says of the Davidic king, 'And I will make him the first-born, the highest of the kings of the earth.' The king is not the first king ever to exist. 'First-born' is a synonym for 'highest of the kings of the earth.'

"That *first-born* means supreme in rank is confirmed by what Paul says in the following verses. Jesus is the agent of all creation (v. 16) and exists before all things (v. 17). He is not classed with the creatures but with the Creator" (Thomas L. Trevethan, *Our Joyful Confidence*, [Downers Grove, Ill.:

InterVarsity Press, 1981], p. 37).

Question 2. Paul states that Jesus is the image of the invisible God. Concerning these words, F. F. Bruce writes: "No reader conversant with the OT scriptures . . . could fail to be reminded of the statement in Gen. 1:26f., that man was created by God 'in his own image.' Defaced as the divine image in man may be by reason of sin, yet in the order of creation it remains true . . . that man is 'the image and glory of God' (1 Cor. 11:7). This image of God in man, moreover, is a copy or reflection of the archetypal image—that is to say, of God's beloved Son" (*Ephesians and Colossians*, pp. 193-94).

The group may want to look at John 14:9-10 for additional help in understanding the phrase "the image of the invisible God."

Question 3. Paul refers to Christ as the Creator of thrones, powers, rulers and authorities (v. 16). In this context he is referring to angels, which figured prominently in the Colossian heresy (see F. F. Bruce, *Ephesians and Colossians*, pp. 198-99). The false teachers believed that God could only be reached indirectly, through an angelic hierarchy. Therefore, they encouraged the worship of angels (2:18) and viewed Christ as only one power among many. Paul refutes this notion by stating that Christ created the very beings the Colossians were tempted to worship. As Creator he alone deserves our worship and allegiance.

Question 4. The "church" (v. 18) refers to all Christians in all ages and places. It is not a denomination or local congregation. If needed, you may want to consider Paul's references to the church as Jesus' body in Romans 12:4-5 and 1 Corinthians 12:12-27.

In recent years there has been considerable debate about the meaning of the word *head*. Traditionally it has been defined as "chief" or "ruler." More recently it has been argued that the word means "source" or "origin." Obviously you will not be able to settle this issue in the few minutes you have for group discussion. However, it is clear from the immediate context of Colossians that Jesus occupies the supreme position in the church, regardless of whether this position is viewed as one of authority or source.

Question 7. Reconciliation applies to bridging over a quarrel or doing away with enmity. The parties being reconciled were formerly hostile to one another. Verse 21 calls us sinners, enemies of God.

The phrase "reconcile to himself all things" (v. 20) has been interpreted by some as teaching universalism, the doctrine that everyone will eventually be saved. However, the consistent teaching of Scripture is that some will be eternally lost (see Mt 25:41-43; Rom 2:8-9, 12; Heb 10:26-31; 2 Pet 2:4-10; Rev 20:11-15). Paul is emphasizing that Christ's salvation will extend to every part of creation. He will bring peace and salvation to both earth and heaven.

Question 9. Allow time to reflect on honest emotional reactions to such an amazing description of Christians. Encourage group members to voice their joy, wonder, doubts, fears or questions. Think about how someone's acceptance and affirmation of you makes you want to be the person they think you are.

Question 10. The group may have difficulty thinking of people who feel a need to be reconciled to God and to be free from accusation. Encourage group members to recall remarks they have heard from their friends. For example, have their friends expressed fears or mentioned that they were under considerable stress? Have they talked about their need for acceptance? Such questions will help them identify subtle and sometimes unspoken needs. Perhaps some might share how they handled their longings for acceptance with God before they became Christians.

Study 4. Colossians 1:24—2:5. Growing Pains.

Purpose: To understand what spiritual maturity includes and to determine to move toward that goal at any cost.

Question 1. When Paul speaks of filling up what is lacking in Christ's afflictions (1:24), he obviously doesn't think there is any deficiency in Christ's atoning sacrifice. Peter O'Brien writes: "Though presently exalted in heaven, Christ continues to suffer in his members, and not least in Paul himself. This was driven home to him on the Damascus road when Christ said to him: 'Why do you persecute me?' (Acts 9:4). Up until this moment, Paul had been actively engaged in making Christ suffer in the person of his followers in Judea. But from now on he would suffer for Christ's sake" (*Colossians, Philemon*, Word Biblical Commentary [Waco, Tex.: Word, 1982], p. 80).

Questions 2-3. A basic principle of Bible study is to discover what a word or idea meant to the author. He may not use the word in the same way as you do today. Be sure to define *mystery* according to what Paul says here.

Paul teaches that all Christians can now understand the mysteries of God. This contradicts the false teachers who claimed to have special revelation.

Question 5. The term *perfect* (1:28) may cause problems. The word, which means "complete, fully developed," can also be translated "mature." Gnostics later used it for those privileged to be initiated into the higher realms of knowledge (*The New Bible Commentary: Revised* [Grand Rapids, Mich.: Eerdmans, 1970], p. 1146).

Notice the repetition of the word *everyone* in verse 28. The Gnostics taught that a deep knowledge of God was reserved for just a few, special

Christians (the "perfect"). Paul, on the other hand, countered their elitist attitude by emphasizing that every believer is one of the "perfect."

Question 6. Encourage the group to reflect on what has helped them to grow spiritually. Be prepared to give some specific examples of how warning, wise teaching, prayer, hard work and depending on Christ's power has helped you to mature in Christ.

Question 7. The words *orderly* and *firm* in verse 5 are military terms. Paul commends the Colossians for being in a military formation that presents a firm front against the deceptive tactics of the enemy. The Colossians have taken their battle stations to combat error (Trevethan, *Our Joyful Confidence,* p. 61).

Question 8. For example, some today claim that one goal of our Christian life should be to achieve financial wealth through Christ. In reality such people are encouraging their followers to pursue a materialistic dream rather than to follow Christ and to fill up what is lacking in his afflictions (1:24).

Study 5. Colossians 2:6-23. No Additions Needed.

Purpose: To understand and enjoy the fullness each believer has when he or she receives Christ.

Question 1. Encourage exploration of each image, though the group may find some more helpful than others. It might help them understand Paul's meaning if they imagine the roots of a tree, a building under construction and a river overflowing its banks. You might mention that *rooted* is in the perfect tense, indicating something that happened in the past (at conversion) but is still true; whereas built up, strengthened and overflowing are in the present tense, indicating an ongoing experience.

Question 2. The heresy Paul confronts was a philosophy centered on mystical knowledge gained by religious ceremonies and rigorous ascetic practices. Its two major sources were human traditions (Jewish influence) and the basic principles of this world (occult and demonic forces). The spiritual was considered good and the physical evil (Trevethan, *Our Joyful Confidence,* pp. 68-74).

Question 3. In verses 9-10 Paul repeats the word *fullness,* which was probably a catchword of the false teachers. "His play on this word is likely a response to the erroneous philosophy besetting the church. His opponents seem to be claiming that Jesus is merely a part of the fullness, the series of emanations from the spiritual world to our material realm. Many other equal or greater spiritual beings and the power of these other lords must somehow be placated or broken. 'Jesus is true,' they might say, 'but hardly sufficient for our needs. We must move ahead to embrace and conquer the fullness'" (Trevethan, *Our Joyful Confidence*, p. 74).

The Bible speaks of spiritual "fulness" as what the human spirit most longs for. This fullness comes only from Christ who was fully God and fully human.

Question 4. Allow time to reflect on the deep needs we usually cover up or fail to recognize. Then look for specific connections with what Jesus has done for us.

A written code (v. 14) was a signed confession listing personal debts. A triumph (v. 15) was "the victory parade given for conquering generals when they returned to Rome. In the victory celebration the defeated enemies, bound in chains, were dragged through the city. Then came the conquering general riding in a chariot, receiving the acclamation of the spectators who benefited from his victory" (Trevethan, *Our Joyful Confidence,* p. 78).

Help the group think about the implications of these verses. Many believers feel unacceptable and condemned by God because of their sinfulness. Their consciences continually accuse them of being unworthy. Such people need to realize that Christ has cancelled every accusation that we or that others might make against us, nailing these accusations to the cross. God now accepts us fully and completely in Christ—not because of who we are but because of what Christ has done.

The powers and authorities that Christ disarmed and humiliated at the cross included all the demonic forces aligned against him. These forces thought they had triumphed by killing the Son of God. However, the moment of their supposed victory was actually the moment of their defeat.

Question 5. Our sins are offensive words or actions that deviate from God's standards. Our sinful nature describes something much deeper—who we are and what we are like in our innermost being. Because our actions are a natural outcome of our nature, our nature must be changed before we can stop sinning. Fortunately Christ has dealt with both our sins and our sinful nature. Our sins have been eternally forgiven (Heb 10:14), and our nature is being transformed into Christ's image by the Holy Spirit (2 Cor 3:18).

Question 6. The group might read the section silently, with each person inserting his or her name. Or you might move around the circle, with each person reading aloud one sentence with his or her name. Then discuss the question.

Question 7. The false teachers claimed that matter was inherently evil. Because God couldn't be directly involved in creation, a whole series of intermediary powers needed to be placated and worshiped. Since the body was evil, it too needed to be treated harshly, to set the person free from its prison. The true way of release was by superior knowledge granted to the initiated, leading to perfection.

Question 9. After the group observes carefully and defines the issues facing the Colossians, encourage them to be specific and thoughtful about what current issues face us. Some may have legalistic backgrounds that either make them feel secure or rebellious. Possible current "shadows" include simple lifestyle, legalism, charismatic gifts as proof of spirituality or anything that acts as a substitute for faith in Christ.

Question 10. F. F. Bruce gives us the following insight into the meaning of the word *receive*. "When Paul says that his readers have 'received' Christ Jesus as their lord, he uses the verb which was specifically employed to denote the receiving of something which was delivered by tradition. In other words, the Colossians have received Christ Himself as their 'tradition,' and this should prove a sufficient safeguard against following 'the tradition of men' (v. 8). Emphasis is laid on the continuity of the transmission of Christian truth; the teaching which has been delivered to them is identical with the apostolic witness. . . . Let them therefore see to it that their way of thought and life conforms continually to this teaching" (*Ephesians and Colossians*, pp. 226-27). Encourage the group to think too about the meanings of Christ ("Messiah") and Lord.

Prayer. First read the hymn silently to appreciate the theme of each verse. Then read it together as a prayer.

Study 6. Colossians 3:1-11. New Life.

Purpose: To make pleasing Christ our ultimate goal rather than pleasing our sinful nature or our culture.

Question 1. Notice that Paul mentions only Christ in heaven as the focus of our hearts and minds. In contrast, the Jewish mystics thought that mystical experiences were the way to heavenly realms.

Question 2. The "things above" are those things related to Christ and to our new life in him. To understand them more fully, however, we must understand Paul's statements about Christ in verses 1-4 and how they apply to us.

Notice first that Christ has been raised and is "seated at the right hand of God" (v. 1). This is in fulfillment of Psalm 110:1, which states: "The lord says to my lord: 'Sit at my right hand until I make your enemies a footstool for your feet.'" In Jewish culture the seat on the right hand was the place of highest honor and, in this case, authority. From that place, Christ is reigning as king over the kingdom he inaugurated during his first coming (see Mk 1:15;

Col 1:13).

Second, notice that although Christ's position and authority are now hidden from the eyes of the world (v. 3), there will come a day when he will appear in glory at his second coming (v. 4). Then the last of his enemies will be vanquished (Ps 110:1), and his kingdom will be fully and eternally established.

Question 3. How does all this apply to us? Because Christ is in us (Col 1:27) and we are in him (2:9), our life is inseparable from his. Just as he died on the cross, we also died with him to our old way of life and to the dominion of darkness in which we lived (1:13; 3:3). Just as he was raised from the dead, so also we were raised with him to a new life and to citizenship in his kingdom (1:12-13; 3:3). And just as he will one day be glorified, we too will be appear with him in glory (3:4).

Therefore, our lives now and in the future should embody the values and goals of Christ's kingdom. As we seek these "things above," we are not retreating from life on earth, because Christ's authority extends to every aspect of our lives (3:12—4:6). Likewise, the "earthly things" we are to avoid are not the daily aspects of life but rather those worldly values and goals that characterized our lives as non-Christians (3:5-9).

Question 4. Be prepared to give a personal example. This can free others to speak honestly.

Question 5. The false teachers adopted the Greek view that the soul is heavenly and eternal, but the body is perishable and so is unimportant. In contrast, Paul emphasizes that it does matter what we do with our bodies.

The group may express confusion about the command to put to death after the previous statement that we have died with Christ. F. F. Bruce writes: "The believer is living on two planes so long as he remains in this mortal body: spiritually he already belongs to the age to come, while temporally he is involved in this present age; spiritually he is united to Christ at God's right hand, while temporally he lives on earth. The new nature imparted by Christ does not effect the immediate annihilation of the old nature inherited from his ancestors; so long as he lives in 'this age,' the 'flesh' persists like a dormant force which may spring into activity at any time. Hence the tension, which does not arise from any inconsistency between Paul's premises and his recognition of the facts of the Christian life, but from well-known conditions of Christian experience" (*Ephesians and Colossians*, p. 269).

Question 6. If needed, you might give examples from the current news of greedy or immoral behavior being rewarded or accepted.

Question 8. If the group misses any of the six items, you might ask about that item specifically.

Paul states that our new self is "being renewed in knowledge in the image of its Creator" (v. 10). For additional background on the image of God, see the leader's notes to study three, question three.

Question 10. Notice what God has already done and is presently doing in us (vv. 9-11). You might contrast that with our best efforts at determination and self-discipline.

Question 11. Encourage the group to think of specific divisions in our culture that the church is to avoid. If needed, ask, "What racial, social, economic or religious differences are represented in your church?"

Study 7. Colossians 3:12-17. New Lifestyle.

Purpose: To understand the character qualities of Christians and ways of responding to other Christians that are consistent with who we are in Christ.

Questions 2-3. Encourage the group to internalize this description, to feel the force of knowing these are titles God gives you. Savor the freedom of knowing you don't earn them.

Question 4. Picture a situation at home or at work where responding with compassion and humility would draw attention because it is uncommon.

Question 5. We usually approach the Bible individually, making personal applications. But this passage speaks about the qualities that affect our relationships to each other. Help the group think about how countercultural these qualities are.

Question 7. "In all inner conflicts as well as in all disputes and differences among Christians, Christ's peace must give the final decision. We are to do nothing that would violate that peace" (Vaughan, *Colossians*, p. 215).

Question 8. Notice the parallelism between letting the word of Christ dwell in us richly (v. 16) and being filled with the Spirit (Eph 5:18-20). Both the Word and the Spirit work together, not only in our individual lives but also in our corporate worship. Our meetings are to be characterized by teaching and admonition based on the word of Christ. Likewise, there must be opportunity for singing "psalms, hymns and spiritual songs."

Question 9. Singing can help the Word of God dwell in us richly. Many Old Testament psalms were sung. Before the New Testament was written, the stories and teachings about Jesus were memorized and passed on from person to person. Sometimes the teachings were set to music and became an important part of Christian worship and education. Second Timothy 2:11 is probably one example.

Question 11. The group may have trouble with the idea of doing something in Jesus' name. In the Bible a name indicated the essential character of a person. Paul has shown that Jesus is Lord of all as the Creator, Sustainer, Redeemer, Reconciler and the One in whom the fullness of deity dwells. So if we do or say something in Jesus' name, it must be consistent with Jesus' character and will. As his representatives we act or speak as he would if he were bodily present.

Question 12. Consider the futility of external rituals and rules to satisfy our deepest longings. In contrast, out of Christ's fullness in us can flow his qualities of compassion, kindness, humility, gentleness, patience, love, peace and thankfulness.

Study 8. Colossians 3:18—4:1. At Home & on the Job.

Purpose: To examine and adopt the attitudes and actions in our various relationships that are consistent with having fullness in Christ.

Question 1. It is important to note that commands are given to both parties in each relationship. The group may not agree that all are addressed to our weaknesses. But defining the agreement or disagreement should clarify the significance of the commands.

Questions 2-3. The word *submit* raises red flags and tempers in our culture. It is important to note that submission doesn't imply inferiority. Jesus Christ was simultaneously equal with the Father and submissive to the Father. Equality and submissiveness can coexist in human relationships. In Greco-Roman culture the gospel brought a unique freedom to women and slaves. But that freedom was not to be misused to discredit the gospel.

Looking back at the behavior described in Colossians 3:5-17 should help the group to define submit and love specifically and practically.

Question 4. Our culture and human nature say, "Be nice to me, and I'll be nice to you." But the passage says, "Do right even when the other person doesn't." The group may need to explore how much their behavior has been influenced by culture.

Question 5. Throughout the ancient world, minor children were expected to obey their parents. Under Roman law even adult children had to obey their fathers. In the Old Testament, God commanded children to honor their parents (Ex 20:12). A rebellious, disobedient son could be put to death (Deut 21:18-21).

Questions 6-7. Encourage specific, realistic ideas of parenting. After negative examples and stories, be sure to end on positive ideas growing out of the right motives.

Questions 8-9. Paul had said there is neither "slave or free, but Christ is all, and is in all" (3:11). Yet the Christian slave and master still lived in a society where inequalities continued. "It must have been bewildering at times for both sides, and threatening too, not only for those within the little Christian communities, but also for those who anxiously looked on, deeply disturbed at what seemed likely to overthrow the stability of their social order" (R. C. Lucas, *The Message of Colossians & Philemon* [Downers Grove, Ill.: InterVarsity Press, 1980], p. 166). Paul instructs slaves and masters to look at their positions and accountability in new ways.

The amount of space Paul devotes to relationships between slaves and masters may be due to the fact that Onesimus, Philemon's runaway slave, was returning to Colossae with the letters of Colossians and Philemon. Paul hoped that his words would help these two brothers in Christ to be reconciled.

Question 10. Help the group consider the value of accountability, especially for an authority figure.

Question 11. Encourage the group to make specific applications to their office, factory, classroom or profession. Remember stay-at-home parents have a vocation too.

Study 9. Colossians 4:2-18. Making the Most of Opportunities.
Purpose: To understand how our words, lives and prayers work together in witnessing, and to understand how we can help and encourage each other.
Question 1. By recalling what you have studied in Colossians and looking at the context here, the group should be able to answer this question.
Question 2. In your preparation use the dictionary to define *devote*. Share it with the group if necessary. Encourage the group to think about its implications for prayer.
Question 4. The application of verses 3-4 requires action. Use this opportunity to develop a pattern of prompt obedience.
Question 5. The word *outsiders* may sound offensive, but it fits Paul's teaching that we are either "in Christ" or outside of Christ. Recognizing this sensitizes us to our responsibility to all those around us.
Question 6. First, discuss what "full of grace" and "seasoned with salt" means in conversation. "This Christian speaking must always be gracious, especially when answers provoke argument. But gracious words can be insipid and dull, so the apostle asks for some seasoning as well. It is too much to equate salt with wit, but it is not too much to say that our answers should compel interest and attention" (Lucas, *Colossians & Philemon*, p. 175).

Then consider the effect this type of speech would have on the non-Christians around you. "How we speak is nearly as important in influencing others as what we say. We are to speak 'graciously,' in a kindly, gentle fashion. There is to be no shrill, strident, overbearing rhetoric associated with the presentation of the message of grace. But this does not imply that our speech will be bland, boring or insipid. It is to be 'salty,' interesting as well as wholesome" (Trevethan, *Our Joyful Confidence*, p. 145).

Question 7. "Know how to answer everyone" implies that people will question Christians. Help the group to think of the difference between accepting openings rather than making them.

Question 8. In preparation list the people and qualities noted. If the group misses one, ask, "What else do you find?" "Or what does verse ____ add?"

Question 9. Try to put yourself in the skin of these people. Allow yourself to feel their emotions.

Question 10. Be sure to include the effort, scope, specific requests and perseverance of Epaphras's praying.

Question 11. If the group needs help in recalling the problems, suggest that they look at the following verses: 1:21-23; 2:2-10, 16-17, 20-23.

Study 10. Philemon 1-25. Mending Fractured Relationships.

Purpose: To discover and be willing to apply principles for mending fractured relationships between Christians.

Question 1. There are a number of facts in the letter that help us reconstruct what took place, especially if we use our imagination to fill in the gaps. Philemon, a resident of Colossae (see Col 4:9, 17), was evidently one of Paul's converts (Philem 19). He and his wife, Apphia (v. 2), along with their son, Archippus (v. 2), were the hosts for a house church in Colossae (v. 2).

One of their slaves, Onesimus, had evidently run away, perhaps stealing something for his journey (vv. 12, 18). (According to Roman law, such an act was punishable by death.) Somehow he ended up in Rome, over a thousand miles from home, and came in contact with Paul. During his visit with Paul, Onesimus became a Christian (v. 10) and began to be of great help to Paul during his imprisonment (vv. 12-13). Now Paul was sending him back to Philemon (v. 12) in hopes of reconciling these two estranged brothers in Christ.

Question 2. Paul especially commends Philemon for his faith and love. Notice that he mentions twice how loving Philemon is (vv. 4, 7). Philemon's love becomes the basis for Paul's appeal in verses 8-10.

Question 3. Christians are required to forgive others because Jesus Christ has forgiven them (Eph 4:32; Col 3:13). Jesus had harsh words to say to those who were unwilling to forgive others (see Mt 18:21-35).

Question 4. In verse 11 Paul uses a play on words to describe Onesimus, whose name means "useful."

Questions 5-6. Half the group might identify with Onesimus and half with Philemon. Give each subgroup time to discuss their feelings, fears and risks. Then have each subgroup respond as Onesimus or Philemon.

Question 7. A mediator intervenes between two parties who are estranged and alienated to bring reconciliation. They need a mediator to help them do what they can not do alone.

Question 8. Again put yourself in the skin of the two men. As you face each other each day, what is different in how you speak or act? What is still the same as before?

Question 9. Encourage the group to state specific principles that would apply to mending current fractured relationships between Christians.

Martha Reapsome is a staff member with Neighborhood Bible Studies, Inc. She is coauthor with her husband, James, of the LifeGuide Bible Study Marriage: God's Design for Intimacy.

What Should We Study Next?

A good place to start your study of Scripture would be with a book study. Many groups begin with a Gospel such as *Mark* (20 studies by Jim Hoover) or *John* (26 studies by Douglas Connelly). These guides are divided into two parts so that if twenty or twenty-six weeks seems like too much to do at once, the group can feel free to do half and take a break with another topic. Later you might want to come back to it. You might prefer to try a shorter letter. *Philippians* (9 studies by Donald Baker), *Ephesians* (11 studies by Andrew T. and Phyllis J. Le Peau) and *1 & 2 Timothy and Titus* (12 studies by Pete Sommer) are good options. If you want to vary your reading with an Old Testament book, consider *Ecclesiastes* (12 studies by Bill and Teresa Syrios) for a challenging and exciting study.

There are a number of interesting topical LifeGuide studies as well. Here are some options for filling three or four quarters of a year:

Basic Discipleship
Christian Beliefs, 12 studies by Stephen D. Eyre
Christian Character, 12 studies by Andrea Sterk & Peter Scazzero
Christian Disciplines, 12 studies by Andrea Sterk & Peter Scazzero
Evangelism, 12 studies by Rebecca Pippert & Ruth Siemens

Building Community
Christian Community, 12 studies by Rob Suggs
Fruit of the Spirit, 9 studies by Hazel Offner
Spiritual Gifts, 12 studies by Charles & Anne Hummel

Character Studies
New Testament Characters, 12 studies by Carolyn Nystrom
Old Testament Characters, 12 studies by Peter Scazzero
Old Testament Kings, 12 studies by Carolyn Nystrom
Women of the Old Testament, 12 studies by Gladys Hunt

The Trinity
Meeting God, 12 studies by J. I. Packer
Meeting Jesus, 13 studies by Leighton Ford
Meeting the Spirit, 12 studies by Douglas Connelly

ALSO FOR SMALL GROUPS...

As well as over 70 titles in the popular *LifeBuilder* series, Scripture Union produces a wide variety of resources for small groups. Among them are:

WordLive – an innovative online Bible experience for groups and individuals offering a wide variety of free material: study notes, maps, illustrations, images, poems, meditations, downloadable podcasts, prayer activities. Log on and check it out: www.wordlive.org

The Multi-Sensory series – popular resources for creative small groups, youth groups and churches, with appeal for a wide range of learning styles and plenty of photocopiable pages.

Deeper Encounter – for confident groups having a good understanding of Bible text, seven sessions in each title complete with CD audio tracks and photocopiable worksheets.

Essential 100 and **Essential Jesus** – 100-reading overviews of the Bible (Essential Bible) and the person and work of Jesus (Essential Jesus), with notes and helps, presented as a programme for individuals, small groups or whole churches.

SU publications are available from Christian bookshops, on the Internet, or via mail order. Advice on what would suit your group best is always available. You can:

- phone SU's mail order line: local rate number 08450 706 006
- email info@scriptureunion.org.uk
- log on to www.scriptureunion.org.uk
- write to SU Mail Order, PO Box 5148, Milton Keynes MLO, MK2 2YX

Scripture Union
USING THE BIBLE TO INSPIRE CHILDREN, YOUNG PEOPLE AND ADULTS TO KNOW GOD